Releasing Creativity in You!!

By Cindy Tiefel

ISBN:
978-1-888081-22-0

Published by

Good News Fellowship Ministries
220 Sleepy Creek Rd
Macon, GA 31210

Format and cover design by Lisa Buck
lisa.joy.buck@gmail.com

Table of Contents

Notes:

Endorsements

"Cindy's book is a personal testimony of the creative power of God that is both compelling and encouraging, and helps to make creativity accessible and desirable to everyone. I received much confirmation and joy just reading it. Now let's go and create!!"
--Julie Sparks
Prophetic Artist for Healing Rooms
Minister to Children

"Get it! Get it! This book will help you "have a go" – You can do all things through Christ. Don't be a woulda, coulda, shoulda Christian. Step up and step out. You might get yourself a surprise at your hidden gifts and talents."
--David Walters
  Author, Minister
  David Walters Ministry

"Cindy's paintings in essence are the voice of God in art. The book explains how this expression of our Father can be displayed in each of us not only through art, but teaching, gymnastics, cooking and whatever passion the Lord has put on our hearts to give to others. Our Lord is a giver and delights to talk to us through our giftings and obedience. We do not necessarily have to be talented, but just bring our lives and obedience to Him and He does the rest.
Make God's dreams your dreams! An inspiring read for sure."

--Toni miller, RN.BSN,
  Healing rooms at Creekside
  Volunteer at St. Vincent

"I love the way Cindy wants everyone to be used in the arts. She is so encouraging. She imparts a "you can do it " attitude.

--Kathie Walters
  Author, Minister
  www.kathiewaltersministry.com

"I was listening to Cindy tell about what the Lord was doing in her life, and I was excited as she told me how God was creating the gift of painting in her life. The excitement and joy you will feel as you read Cindy's book will encourage you in ways that you may have thought impossible, but with God all things are possible."

  --Beverly Pickering

Cindy is a dear friend of mine and I love how she trusts God and allows Him to use her for His glory and blessing of others! In this book she helps the reader to see they don't have to have to rely on natural talent to be creative with God. Simple obedience to His voice releases Him to use us in creative ways and to allow His beauty to shine in what we do! Cindy lives this truth in all she does! She shows how simple and easy it is to be creative and also shows the variety of expressions of creativity in this book! I have watched God speak through her through the paintings she does in The Healing Rooms we do. Her joy in the process is contagious and inspiring!

--Patricia Foxworth
Director of Healing Rooms/Hope Center
Creekside Church
Fishers, IN

Releasing the Creativity Inside You is an insightful book about the Creator's gifts inside His children. Cindy gives simple yet realistic examples of God's creative nature inside you. This book describes how you can limit God or agree with Him and let His creativity flow though you to influence the world around you. You'll enjoy Cindy Tiefel's creative side as you tiptoe through the pages of this exciting book.

--Bonnie Jones
Bob & Bonnie Jones Ministries
Fort Mill, SC

Notes:

What is Creativity?

Creativity is the ability or power to create. Human beings are creative beings according to one dictionary. Another dictionary says,

> "The ability to make new things or think of new ideas."

And still another definition states creativity as,

> "Relating to or involving the imagination or original ideas, especially in the production of an artistic work." Or, "A person who is creative."

What does Father God, creator of all Heaven and Earth, have to say about Creativity?

In the Bible in Genesis it says that God created the Heavens and the earth. (Genesis 1:3) And God said, "Let there be light," and there was light. God made a declaration, He spoke, and there was light!

In Genesis 1:26 God said,

> "Let us make mankind in our image, in our likeness, so that they may rule."

Genesis 1:27,

> "So God created (spoke) mankind in His own image, in the image of God He made them; male and female He created them."

Job 22:28,

> "You will decree a thing, and it will be established for you, and light will shine on your ways."

Proverbs 18:21,

> "The tongue has the power of life and death, and those who love it will eat of its fruit."

So we can conclude from this that we are made in God's image, and because He is a creative God, we too are creative beings. All of us are creative beings therefore we have the ability to create. You say, "Not me!" Well are you sure?...Let me explain further.

The Monarch and the Hibiscus

It was May of 2014 and my husband and I were on a Caribbean vacation. As I soaked in the sun, I felt a strong presence of the Lord come upon me.

I then saw a vision of a Monarch butterfly and a red Hibiscus flower and tears began to roll down my face.

When I asked the Lord about the vision, He had me look up the meaning of "Monarch." My handy Webster dictionary said, "Hereditary ruler," "King", "Queen", "A large butterfly of North America, having black edged orange wings." The Hibiscus? Well I knew that was a very beautiful, red flower which I had seen for the first time in Maui! The Spiritual meaning of Hibiscus is "opportunity." Red meaning, "Blood Covenant." This is all about opportunity. "Climb every mountain...follow every rainbow 'til you find your dream." This is the dream that God has put in your heart and as His child, this is your inheritance.

Then the Lord spoke to me and said,

> "I am restoring Creativity and Beauty back to
> My Church."

It was just two years before, in May of 2012, that the Lord gave me a vision of a room filled with beautiful, pink-lavender water lilies. The water lily meaning "perfect beauty."

Over the next few weeks, after the water lily vision, I was told several times that I had the gift of creativity. "What did this mean?" I wondered. I even had two people go so far as to tell me that I was to paint my visions. I wasn't an artist, and although I loved to sing and dance, I was fairly certain that no one wanted to hear or see me do either. Paint the visions that I see? The problem was, although I love art, I couldn't paint....or so I thought!

What was this Gift of Creativity?

In June 2012, I was at The First International Creative Conference at my church in Indianapolis. The Lord had told me to attend, so there I was, wandering around the lobby looking at the many books that were for sale regarding the Arts. Why did the Lord want me to attend this conference? It was only down the street from my house, and at the time I was attending that church... so okay I showed up.

As I wandered around the lobby looking at books I was wondering where everyone was. I picked up a book titled, <u>Born to Create</u> by Theresa Dedmon. Just as I was looking at this book I heard a voice from behind the stack of books say, "If you purchase that book, I can sign it for you." I was a bit startled as I did not realize any one else was there. I agreed and as I was watching Theresa Dedmon, Head of the Prophetic Arts Department at Bethel Church in Redding, CA, sign my book, I said, "I don't know why I am here". With out looking up or missing a beat she said, "Because you are supposed to paint the visions that you see!" Okay, now this was getting crazy! I protested, "But I can't paint!" She quickly responded, "Oh, that has nothing to do with it!" The fact that I can't paint has nothing to do with it....??? She wasn't being moved by my protests in any way. She explained that I needed to attend her workshop later that day. There, she prayed for me to not only receive an impartation to activate **my** creativity, but all that **she** was carrying too. I didn't really feel anything, but I have been that told that you don't need to feel something to receive it. Although I usually felt things, I received this one by faith. Then Theresa said, "don't leave!". She wanted her assistant to pray for me. As her assistant prayed for me I saw a huge fireball come to me and I fell to the floor. Well if I wasn't sure before, now I was now certain I received something! WOW!

In Theresa's workshop, she explained that creativity is anything you create with your mouth, or your hands or body, and is not limited to artists, musicians, singers, and dancers - those we think of as creative. These are all beautiful examples of creativity, but we are not limited to just these areas.

She was expanding our minds by saying that a hairdresser, a manicurist, and a chef preparing a meal are all creative. Someone who acts, writes a book or poetry, builds a house, a fashion designer, an interior decorator, a gardener, a scientist with an idea, a computer designer, a tattoo artist, a brick mason, even someone speaking an encouraging word over you or laying hands on you to pray are all examples of creativity. These are all expressions of our Heavenly Father.

God is the Creator and His Spirit is in you, so you also have the power to create! Because your words are creative.

So when you speak you are creating a pathway to walk in!

Notes:

Painting my Visions!

"Don't despise the time of small beginnings", I kept hearing.

I was sitting there, having my time with the Lord and trying to draw with markers and colored pencils. As I tried to draw my visions, I couldn't help but think, "These look like a 6 year-old drew these." The clincher was when I was finished the Lord would say, "post it on Facebook!" "What? You have got to be kidding me! Post these on Facebook?" I wasn't even comfortable looking at them myself, let alone posting them on Facebook. But I have learned it is best to just do what He says, so I posted them against my own judgment.

I lived through that, as I wasn't even sure if anyone saw the posts. It seemed as if there might have been a couple of people who did "like" them. Ha Ha! I secretly think the Lord told a few people to like them to encourage me.

At church I became part of a prophetic prayer team. It was myself and one other person named Carrie. She did it three Sundays a month and I did it one Sunday. I would sit at a table in the lobby and people asked me to pray for them. As I got a vision, I would scribble it on a piece of paper. Most didn't seem to care about my lack of artistic ability but were more interested in the visions I had for them. I had no idea what these visions meant, but as I drew them and explained what I was seeing, people were saying "Wow!!" One Sunday, I had a line of people waiting until 3 PM for me to pray for them. Little did I know that most of them were ARTISTS! I would just like to say **"Thank-you!"** to those artists whom looked beyond my lack of artistic ability to see what the Lord was saying to them.

Later that summer, as I was still making my feeble attempts to draw what the Holy Spirit spoke to me, He told me how to draw a butterfly. In ten minutes I drew two butterflies. They looked pretty good, for me at least! I was happy there was progress!

Later, I had meetings with ladies at my home and the Holy Spirit asked me to set this painting out. I didn't know why but I did as He asked. Some of the ladies started receiving emotional healing. I decided to take my butterfly drawing to church during the prophetic prayer time. People wept over "The Butterflies" drawing. One lady said that it caused something from her childhood to come up; a nun told her that people don't talk to Jesus. She was broken-hearted because as a child, she talked to Him all the time. We prayed together for her to be healed of that wound. One man just wept uncontrollably over the drawing. I never knew what that was about, but I sensed that it was something he was unable to speak about. As he was weeping, I just gently prayed as the Holy Spirit led me. Another time a lady saw the drawing of the two butterflies and said something about a restorer and threw herself to the ground crying in front of it. I didn't really understand what was going on, but the Holy Spirit knew exactly. I started to understand a bit more and knew it had nothing to do with me. It was all about the Holy Spirit.

In July of 2013, a friend of mine, Patty, and her husband, Ron, were leading The Healing Rooms at our church. She asked me to paint at The Healing Rooms. Of course I said "yes" because I felt the Lord wanted me to do it, but as the date got closer I became nervous. Every time I would mention that I can't paint, others would say, "Don't say that!" Finally, I couldn't take it any longer and I said to the Lord, "I know you want me to do this but I just don't know how to paint!" He said, **"I know you don't know how to paint but you know the One who does. You'll get up there on that stage with *your childlike faith and your courage and I will teach you to paint."***

It was right after that I had made the trip out to The Bethel Healing rooms. While in their creative room, I saw the beautiful Caribbean blue/green eyes of Jesus. To this day I still do not know the full meaning of seeing His eyes, but I am excited to find out!

I had never even used a paintbrush before, so before the first Healing Room the Lord told me that I could finger paint. I also used a couple of sponges. As I got up there to paint I felt the Holy Spirit guiding me every step of the way. He would even tell me pick up certain colors and do this or that. The pastor was there and thanked me for the atmosphere of peace. That was encouraging to me. I made it through and I even painted two paintings. Every two weeks, the challenge was "What was I going to paint?" The Lord always showed me, and as I trusted him more and more with that, He would give me the paintings ahead of time. At times I had others tell me they saw an angel with me as I painted. Still, I struggled with my natural artistic ability to paint even as well-meaning people would pray for me to increase in my ability. The atmosphere at church was great to paint in and not the same as at my house. I simply just enjoyed painting in the Lord's presence and stopped caring so much about my ability. It was a bit tough when really gifted people would paint such beautiful paintings along side me, but I know the Lord was working on me to not care what other people think. I did have a couple of people who purchased my paintings because they spoke to them in some way, which was very encouraging to me. Each time the Holy-

Spirit revealed something new to me, I received a new healing.

One day while painting in The Healing Rooms, there was a lady who was, for all general purposes, blind. You could actually see a film like substance over her eyes and she walked with assistance and a special cane. That day I was painting a prophetic clock that the Lord had showed me months before. He said, "Today is the day to paint this." As I was painting, the blind lady was up front worshipping with some of the ladies from The Healing Room and they were praying for her. I was on the stage painting and the lady started saying that she could see my painting. The lady said, "Yes. I recognize and can see God's prophetic clock." The other ladies thought she was getting healed of her blindness. The lady kept trying to explain she wasn't. The Holy Spirit spoke to me and told me that this lady could barely see in the natural, but she could see quite well in Heaven. After I finished, I went and spoke with this lady. She confirmed what Holy Spirit had spoken to me - that she could not see in the natural, but could see quite well in the supernatural. I asked her to pray for me. I don't know what happened to that painting of the prophetic clock. I haven't seen it since that day.

I am very thankful for the church I attend to recognize my creative gifting in my paintings, in spite of my lack of artistic ability. My church hasn't really said much about my paintings, however they have hung many of them on the church walls in the main sanctuary. That says a lot to me. The pastor of the church is quite artistically gifted and for him to allow my paintings to hang on the walls of the church - well that honors me. Thank-you!

Creative Healing

Along the way, the Lord revealed to me that my creativity had been cut off by others and by my own negative thoughts.

One day I was walking across my kitchen and the Holy Spirit showed me two of my kindergarten teachers that had spoke some critical words over me regarding a Thanksgiving picture I had drawn as a child. They criticized my use of scissors, which resulted in a timeout instead of playtime. The Holy Spirit said that is where my artistic ability was shutdown. I remember the situation. I don't really remember being upset about it or anything, but at age 53, I clearly remembered this happening. The Holy Spirit led me through a prayer of forgiveness and release of that negativity.

Another time the Lord showed me when I had been a baton twirler around the age of seven. I guess I had been quiet good at it. I was even taking private lessons, but I never remembered being told I was good. I just thought I was having fun. I just remember being asked if I wanted to take private lessons and my mom said yes. After a while it seemed more like work and not so much fun. Years later my mom told me that I was really good and asked me why I didn't pursue it more. I told her that I had no idea I was any good, so there was another prayer.

The Lord showed me that as a young girl, I had an interest in sewing, but only on two occasions (except for Home Economics class) did I ever have anyone teach me how to sew. In my mid 20's, I bought myself a sewing machine and practiced making clothes for my young son, and curtains at my house. My son waited until he was older to tell me how embarrassed he was to wear my creations, lol! I was also into stenciling. It was all over the walls and my curtains. Because the outfits I made and my stenciling were not perfect, the looks I received from others bothered me. I thought if my creations weren't perfect, then I should just give up. God never wants us to do anything out of perfection or performance. He just wants us to enjoy what we are doing. The goal is to have fun. So I asked Him to forgive me for my perfection and performance issues.

There was also a time when I was singing kind of loudly in front of others, and someone gave me a weird look. One of those unspoken looks. I felt condemned and humiliated. Yes, again I needed to forgive them, and again to deal with my performance and perfection issues. Another prayer.

As a child I always wanted to be a June Taylor dancer. I loved dancing! My mom was young and had other things going on, so I was never able to take dance lessons. By the time I figured out that I might be talented enough to be a June Taylor Dancer, I was told that I was too old and it was too late. I think maybe I wasn't supposed to go down that road, but I do still enjoy dancing - especially before the Lord.

The Lord revealed to me that He wanted me to step out and maybe sing a little song to minister to others. Although I am not a terrible singer, no one wants to hear me sing. So this was quite a stretch for me. I was in a group for a brief time and we would go out to minister to others. One time while ministering downtown, the Lord kept giving me songs to sing to those whom we were ministering to. There was a man and lady who were the leaders of the group. The lady was all for it and was helping me sing these songs. However, later, when others weren't around, the man criticized me for doing this. This really shook me up for a bit. The Lord said, "Shake it off, forgive, and move on!"

Notes:

Let's choose to Forgive

You can see that I had many areas of creativity, but criticism, lack of encouragement, my desire for perfection, and my performance issues kept me from living those out at a much younger age. As you are reading this, you may have some similar issues come up. If so, let's pray a prayer to forgive others and yourself, because you are never too old to start having fun with God!

Please pray out loud this prayer or your own prayer:

_____

Dear Heavenly Father,

Please help me to forgive, from my heart, all those who criticized me, and failed to encourage me, of their or my own demands of performance and perfection. Forgive me Lord for wanting the praises of man. Forgive me Lord for taking something You meant for fun and making it hard.

Oh Lord restore to me all my creative gifts - the ones I know about and the ones I don't. Holy Spirit, I give You permission to show me any other areas of creativity that need to be healed.

In Jesus name. Amen

Decree and Declare a Thing

Job 22:28: "You can decree a thing and it will be established to you; and light will shine on your ways."

One way we can all create, as we have been discussing, is by speaking words or singing songs that bring **life and encouragement**. Another way is by praying prayers and laying on of hands to pray for others.

I would like to thank my friend Nancy, who many years ago turned to this scripture (Job 22:28) and it just stuck with me. Until most recently, I haven't totally understood what I was doing, and probably still don't, but we can pray powerful prayers that can move mountains by decreeing and declaring.

Many years ago I discovered that if I was depressed or down, I could just speak scriptures out loud. Then I started saying them *for me and to me*. I started to feel so much better, that I would do that when ever I felt down. I had no idea what I was doing. I just knew that I liked it and I felt better when I did it.

After a while, I would pray them over not just me, but my family, then adding all my generations. For example I would pray:

> "No weapons formed against me, or my family, or all my generations will prosper and we will refute every tongue that accuses us. That is the promise and my inheritance from the Lord."

or

> "The Lord has not given me, or my family, or all of my generations a spirit of fear but of power, love and a sound mind." or "The joy of the Lord is my, my family, and all my generations strength!"

They say there are over 7,000 promises in the Bible that God wants us to come into agreement with, and speak over ourselves, our families, and our generations. As we speak these promises over ourselves, our families, and our generations, we start believing what we are saying, and at some point we step over into God's faith.

Hebrews 11:1,

> "Now Faith is the assurance of things that we hope for, and assurance about what we do not see."

I found out in recent years that decreeing and declaring is a high-level of intercession. Something that made me feel good and comforted me at times by realizing God had a higher purpose!

Father in Heaven, Holy is Your name, Your
Kingdom Come Your
will be done on Earth
as it is in Heaven!

In early December of 2004, a man by the name of Bruce Wilkinson, author of the book, The Prayer of Jabez, came to my church. I was familiar with his book and others he had written. I assumed that he came to our church to speak about another one of his books.

As Mr. Wilkinson started to speak, he began telling about living in South Africa with his family and how many of the people were starving over there. He was starting a Mission Trip called "Dream for Africa". He was asking for volunteers to go over to South Africa to help him with his mission. I wasn't really interested in going on a mission trip, however the Lord had other thoughts about that. The Lord spoke to me and said,

> "I want you to take that little bit of money that you have from when your Father passed away a few years ago and use it to go on this mission trip."

I didn't want to go...long story short. I argued. The Lord won. I ask Him why He wanted me to go on this trip and He told me that He wanted me to be a well-rounded Christian. Several hundred people, myself included, went forward when Mr. Wilkinson asked who would go. But when it came time to go in March 2005, less than a third actually went.

South Africa

We flew into and stayed in Johannesburg ("JoBurg") for short. We stayed in a very nice hotel, similar to a Hampton Inn, but with full dining and laundry services. Our mission trip was to an area of town called a "Township".

We were at one of the townships where all those who were black had to live. You could work in the city, but it was my understanding that, with little exception, if you were black in Johannesburg - you had to live in this one particular township or one like it.

They took us into this township by bus, and up until we arrived, no white people (except for the police) had ever been there before. They took us to a church and it was there that we were divided into groups. Each group was given a person from the township to help us and to trans-late for us. Most people spoke English, but some did not. We were told to go with our group to each home, offer prayer, and plant a small garden for them. They wanted the people there to not just have something given to them, but to learn to grow their own food.

Of course in this township there were different areas. We could only go to the nicest homes, because in the really bad areas is they would likely kill us - so we were told. A nice home consisted of a block home with two rooms. The living room/kitchen with a curtain separating it from a small room with a bed, and another room that was a small washroom with a toilet. Most had a TV and electri-city. We could see the really bad area off in the distance. Those homes had four pieces of metal with a curtain over the front so you could not see directly in. The roads we walked on were just rough dirt piled with trash.

Our group was assigned two guides, Connie and Wiseman. Wiseman was a young black man, all of about 19 years of age. He wore a tuxedo every day. He wanted very much to be a pastor. Connie was a nice lady from the church. On the first day, our group went to about 38 homes. My team had elected me to pray for each person while the other members of the team started planting the gardens, with the owner's permission. At the end of the day, we were tired and worn out. My brain was tired from praying for people all day. We all thought 38 homes/gardens was all we could do in a day. To our surprise the leaders said, "Oh no. We want you to do 138 per day." We were stunned! How could we do more, let alone 138 homes in a day? We had three more days to find out. They told us that as people accepted Christ, or said they were Christians and wanted to help us, that we could allow them. I asked the Lord, "How can I pray for all these people and all of their needs?" He said, "Pray the Lord's prayer." I replied, "Just pray the Lord's prayer?" These people had so many needs and wanted me to pray for everything, like I was their only hope. The Lord said, "Just pray whatever they want and then pray the Lord's prayer!" I thought I can do that!

So by the second day we started collecting followers - those who wanted to help us. We were making progress with more homes. The hotel packed a lunch for all of us who were staying at the hotel. As we stopped to take a break and eat our lunch, I questioned our guides and others about their lunches. They said they had no lunch. In fact, they said they had not even eaten that day, nor did they know when they would eat next. We had about twenty following us. There were five of us with lunches and about 25 people to feed. We prayed and then we shared our lunches. Everyone had more than enough to eat and there was some left over! We were all very happy! We knew what the Lord had done.

With thoughts of our recent miracle still fresh on our mind, and with everyone following us, we still needed to be faster in order to cover more homes, so we decided to split up. The four others with my group went with some locals while my group consisted of Connie, Wiseman, myself and a couple of locals who were planting gardens. The Holy Spirit prompted me to ask Connie and Wiseman if they were baptized in the Holy Spirit. They said yes, but the rest of our group was not. So as the three of us started praying for people, the dynamics of the prayers changed. Now people wanted prayer for healings and deliverance, not just prayer for family members and provision. I continued to do as the Lord asked. I lifted up their prayer and ended with the Lord's prayer and as we did that people started getting healed. I had no training in healing, only my experience being healed of Leukemia and stomach issues several years before.

One lady had just had a baby a few days before and was suffering from an infection. After we prayed for her she said, "Hey! I am healed!". Another man chased us down the road saying, "Hey! I got healed!" We didn't even know enough to ask them about their healing. We just prayed what they wanted us to pray and I prayed the Lord's prayer.

There were many homes in which witch doctors lived. They would take the vegetables, but would not allow me near them, especially not to pray for them. We had many that manifested demons around us, appearing to be drunk and speaking in their native language. After we got back to the church, they explained that many of those people were saying that I had to leave and I wasn't wanted there. At no time while we were there was I afraid, which was really unusual for me because I was afraid for a lot less back home. I knew that the Lord was with me and protecting me.

We also went to an area of the township where there was an AIDS clinic that was fully funded by Jerry Springer. I was shocked. The people there said many would have died had it not been for Jerry Springer and his generous funding of this AIDS Clinic. We prayed for many very sick people in that area. At the end of the day after going back to the church we finally reached our goal of 138 homes in a day. The church said they were going to check where we had been praying as many were reporting that they were healed! I didn't understand why people were getting healed. I only knew that Holy Spirit had told me what to do and I did it. I spoke and heaven came to earth. The Spirit in me came into agreement with the Word and heaven came. If I can do it, you can do it! I had zero expectation of people getting healed. I had no training. I just prayed for heaven to come and it did! Thank-You Jesus!

I kept in contact with Connie for a while until she moved away. Wiseman and I are in still in contact today. He did become a pastor and is currently a pastor of two churches in South Africa. We have kept in contact all these years. We text and email frequently. I have two natural born sons and I consider Wiseman my third son. I hope to see him again some day before we go home to heaven.

Creative Writing

I always felt I had trouble communicating with others in the written word, especially in emails. People frequently misunderstand me and I felt that because I did not go to college, I was lacking in this area. I did have schooling outside of college, such as Real Estate school, which I passed and got my license, and some medical courses I took to assist with some of my jobs in the medical field. One day, the Lord explained to me that I needed to stop speaking negatively over myself in this area. He said, "You do have a creative writing gift." He reminded me of the poem that He gave me after the death of my mother, which was read at her funeral.

My mother was diagnosed with Inflammatory Breast Cancer at the age of 49. Most die within a year of this type of cancer. I was only in my early 30's at the time and we had not been that emotionally close due to the proximity of our ages. I hit my knees crying out for God to save her. I said, "Lord I am not ready yet." I was a Christian, but had been through two divorces and was not living my life for the Lord at that time. My mother did recover, but only for it to come back three and a half years later. It eventually took her life at age 54.

At that time, I had worked for a surgeon and we shared an office with another surgeon who specialized in Breast Cancer. As I spoke to this surgeon about my mother's initial diagnosis, and all that had happened to her after, he said to me that he had never heard of anyone with Inflammatory Breast Cancer living much more than a year or so, let alone almost six years. Thank-you Jesus for hearing my prayer and giving me those extra years! Although our relationship was never perfect, we did become closer and my mom recommitted her life to Christ three months before her death. One of the pastors from the church I attended at that time came to visit my mom almost every week until she passed. He spoke at her funeral.

Almost immediately after my mom had passed the Lord gave me this poem to comfort me. It was read at her funeral. Here it is:

IF YOU KNEW MY MOTHER

"IF YOU KNEW MY MOTHER"
  YOU KNEW HER AS CAROL. SHE HAD BIG DARK EYES

AND COULD SPICE UP ANY STORY WITH HER EN-
THUSIASM, HER FACIAL EXPRESSIONS AND HER HANDS.

"IF YOU KNEW MY MOTHER"
      YOU'D KNOW THAT SHE LOVED TO READ. I NEVER
SAW ANYONE WHO COULD READ THREE BOOKS AT ONE
TIME BUT MY MOTHER COULD. SHE COULD DO THE
DAILY CROSSWORD PUZZLE ALMOST AS GOOD AS MY
GRANDPA.

"IF YOU KNEW MY MOTHER"
         YOU'D KNOW THAT SHE LOVED HISTORY AND
ANTIQUES, AND I KNOW THAT SHE LOVED TO DREAM OF
THE PEOPLE AND THE STORIES THAT WENT WITH THEM.

"IF YOU KNEW MY MOTHER"
      YOU'D KNOW THAT SHE LOVED MUSIC AND MOVIES.
AS A YOUNG GIRL SHE THOUGHT ELVIS WAS "KING" BUT
IN MORE RECENT YEARS SHE THOUGHT TINA TURNER
COULD ROCK WITH THE BEST OF THEM.

"IF YOU KNEW MY MOTHER"
      YOU'D KNOW THAT SHE LOVED THE HOLIDAYS AND
BIRTHDAYS. SHE WAS AT HER BEST WHEN SHE PLANNING
AND PREPARING OUR FAMILY GET TOGETHERS. SHE
LOVED FOR US TO PLAY CARD GAMES AND MORE
RECENTLY YATZEE AND SHE LOVED TO ROOT FOR THE
PACERS, THE COLTS AND EVEN BOB KNIGHTS IU.

"IF YOU KNEW MY MOTHER"
      YOU KNEW THAT SHE BECAME A WIFE AND A MOTHER
A VERY YOUNG AGE BUT SHE DIDN'T LET THAT STOP
HER

FROM BECOMING A VERY SUCCESSFUL BUSINESS WOMAN.

"IF YOU KNEW MY MOTHER"
   YOU'D KNOW THAT SHE WAS QUITE PRIVATE WITH HER INNER FEELINGS, BUT I SAW HER SHED A TEAR OR TWO WHEN THE ORCHESTRA PLAYED THE "STAR SPANGLED BANNER", AND WHEN THE MINISTER AT CHURCH ON EASTER SAID, "COME TO JESUS IF YOU HAVE CANCER".

"IF YOU KNEW MY MOTHER"
   YOU'D KNOW THAT SHE WAS DIAGNOSED WITH CANCER AT THE YOUNG AGE OF 49 AND THAT SHE FOUGHT THE GOOD FIGHT UP UNTIL THE VERY END.

"IF YOU KNEW MY MOTHER"
   YOU'D KNOW THAT SHE FLOWED OVER OUR LIVES LIKE A WARM GENTLE BREEZE, AND WHEN HER LIFE WAS DONE ON THIS EARTH IT WAS LIKE THE TITLE TO HER FAVORITE MOVIE, SHE WAS GONE…..***GONE WITH THE WIND.***

I have never read this poem with dry eyes, but I don't really know why, as my mother is in Heaven having a great time with other family members who have gone on to be with the Lord.

The Lord had given me one other poem for my grandmother. The passing of my mom was quite hard on my grandmother. One thing led to another and my grandmother wasn't speaking to me for about a year. One day, the Lord gave me a poem and instructed me to send that to her. I don't have that poem, but know after that, we were reunited again.

I didn't share this story much because I have always felt that I wasn't a teacher and didn't want to be one either. Then one day Jesus said, "I am a teacher". I repented for those words. The Lord would frequently tell me to tell others this story or that story in order to help them. A storyteller is also another word for teacher.

So never say you can't do something or you don't want to do something. Look! Now I am writing a book and telling stories...who knew? **Jesus knew!**

Notes:

The Power of Encouraging Words!

Many years ago, I was in a small group of Christians: Nancy, Frank, Steve, and myself. They were, and still are, very powerful Christians and active in their gifting. I had no idea why the Lord wanted me included in this group and I know they wondered about it too. One day they all put their hands on me and imparted the baptism of the Holy Spirit to me. I will never forget that day and I am very thankful that they did that.

Steve, who was normally a man of few words, said that my whole family would be saved including all my brothers and sisters and all of their children. That really opened my mind up and helped me to see them as God sees them. Since then, one of my brothers and his entire family have received Jesus, as well as my sister and two of her children. I know that all of them will come into the Kingdom, as I have received many words after that for my whole family.

Frank gave me a written word about my husband and my two sons - about how God has a great plan for them. They have all received Jesus to date and even though they are still not sure of how that will look for them personally, I know I have hope and can trust Jesus to work out all of the details. Those encouraging words caused me to look at my whole family in a different light.

Around this same time, after many encounters with Jesus showing up and healing me of so much, Jesus started showing up at my house. One day as I sat on my sun porch, Jesus came to me with the Father. The Father spoke to me and said,

> "I am your Heavenly Father, Creator of all of heaven and earth. Jesus is your example and Holy Spirit is how we communicate."

I think He felt I needed that for clarification. After some deliverance and healing from Jesus, He started pulling all of this dark, string-like stuff out of me. For many years after that the Father and I had many fun encounters. The Father told me that if all I ever did was tell people how much He loved them, that I will have done what He wanted me to do. Which leads me to my next story:

It was in November of 2014, or maybe it was 2015 (time goes so fast!). A young lady named Christa was ministering to young boys and girls at the Juvenile Center in our city. She started a ministry and several of us took a special class so we could go to the Juvenile Center with her. Christa had been incarcerated at the Juvenile Center herself as a kid, and gave her life to Jesus after that. She wanted to give back and help those who started out just like her. So this one particular Saturday, she and I went down to the Juvenile Center. I have to say it was quite intimidating as we were locked in with 15-17 year old boys in their cell area. There was only one corrections officer locked in with us. They were monitoring the TV screens, but it was still kind of intimidating.

Christa brought them treats and Bibles with testimonies from different athletes who had received Christ. I brought a DVD and a couple of my paintings with scriptures on them, which I left there afterwards. The Lord said, "Sit there and just enjoy yourself. Don't make plans to say anything or do anything." Christa had much compassion for these boys. They loved the treats and they absolutely loved the DVD, "Father of Lights". They could relate to it. The whole time I could feel the Father's heart for them radiating out of me. After the movie, many of these boys asked if we could bring it again next time. Christa said yes and she passed out the Bibles to anyone who wanted one, including the corrections officer. Christa looked at me and said, "Do you want to say anything?" I told them that I saw greatness in that room that their Heavenly Father loved them. They just kind of looked at me, stunned. Christa looked at me and said "Well I guess we should go now." But the Holy Spirit in me had other plans. He said, "Who wants to receive Jesus? Raise your hand." About half of them raised their hands. Then the Holy Spirit spoke through me and said, "Stand up if you want to receive Jesus." All but one boy stood, although he had raised his hand. Christa prayed over them and I led them in a prayer to received Jesus into their hearts! Every one of them received Jesus. Christa and I looked at each other stunned. We had not expected this. These boys came up to us and shook our hands and thanked us. It was all because of the Love of the Father for these Boys. As we left, Christa said that these boys were the worst offenders. I was shocked. Any one of these boys could have been my own son. A few years before, it had been one of my sons. Not in that jail, and certainly not a worst offender, but for some minor stuff. I knew that the Father Loved them and I often pray for them and wonder how their lives are now.

The Father wants you to know that NO MATTER WHAT YOU HAVE DONE...that He LOVES YOU with an EVERLASTING LOVE!! He created you for a purpose! Dare to find out what that purpose is - give Him your life and live His dream. It is only then that you will you gain your life!

Hope and the Purple Flower

Last October, a friend of mine sent me a YouTube video of Kathie Walters teaching on Seers and Prophets in the UK. I watched Seers and Prophets I and II. It was so good, I watched it several times. On the third time watching this video, a fire went up my right hand, up my arm, across my back, and down my left arm. I saw in the Spirit, a large ball of fiery sticks. I then fell on the floor, rolling around and shaking and I heard the Lord say, "More joy to you and crazy sustainable hope!" I even sent a text to my friend and told her about it. She said she could feel the fire through my text. Over the next several weeks this fire came on me during The Healing Rooms and during worship at church.

It was last May that I emailed Kathie Walters to ask her about a book. As many of you may know, and for those that don't, Kathie will personally reply to you. So as Kathie was replying to my email, she asked me where I was? She said that she needed to come here. I explained where I was at in the world and we began to make arrangements for her to come to my city in July and again in August.

As we made plans and prepared for Kathie's arrival, some of us were in intercession for the conference. As we were praying, I saw in the Spirit, a closed, purple flower drop down from heaven. This purple flower began to open up. As it began to open, a blue flame was in the center. One of the other intercessors seemed to know immediately what this was about. It was about our State waking up with revival. Our state flower is the Peony and the state Bird is the Cardinal. The Peony means "hidden" and one of the many meanings for Cardinal is "hope"!

Myself and another lady named Cindy went to the airport to pick up Kathie and her friend Beverly. Kathie was getting emails from some who follow her ministry; something about a purple flower. I explained that during intercession I had a vision of the purple flower and my friend Cindy had interpreted its meaning. In our Healing Rooms I had painted a picture of this purple flower and we had it displayed at our meeting with Kathie in July.

This had given many people hope about our region and our state - as many leaders seemed to overlook us. At Kathie's August conference, she kept being directed by the Holy Spirit to talk about revival as she felt it was coming upon us soon. Many who attended those conferences were greatly encourage by what Kathie had to say. Her husband David came in August and spoke as well, which was also greatly encouraging. Kathie had revealed a strategy to us about taking back our city. Only God could use a simple purple flower to reveal his hope! Thank-you Kathie and David Walters for coming to our region and agreeing with the Holy Spirit and releasing hope in our area.

Notes:

48

Other Areas of Creativity

There are other areas of creativity aside from the ones we normally think of. For example, a chef cooking a meal. While to many this might not seem like creativity, or maybe not the same kind as music or art, however you might change your mind if you knew some of their stories.

There was a commercial on TV in my local area of a Chef talking about his experience cooking at a nursing home. The Chef is explaining how he was speaking with one of the residence who was feeling a little depressed. The man was explaining to Chef how he just didn't want to be there anymore. The Chef explained that he just made a nice meal and maybe that would help. Later on when Chef stopped to talk with the resident again, he stated that the meal was so good that he thought he might be around a little longer. The Chef was surprised later to learn that the man had just lost his wife. The Chef said that after that day, he looked at his job in a whole new light and just maybe his job was a little more important than he had thought.

I was watching a National News show and as I was getting ready to turn off the TV, I felt the prompting of the Holy Spirit to wait a moment and listen to this story. It seems that one of the associates on the show has a special needs child. That child has been seeing an occupational therapist for ten years. They were doing a segment on this therapist and how she had changed the life of this child. They explained that this woman had wanted to be an occupational therapist since she was in the 7th grade so she could help special needs children. This was a very moving story and the person reporting it said that this was truly a calling and that they were so very grateful to this person for how much they had helped their son.

I don't know about you, but I love to watch the shows where they buy older or repossessed homes and fix them up. It is amazing to me the condition they find these homes in, and then completely re-do them. Even decorating the new home with the homebuyer's furniture. Some buy these homes and you can tell they don't see any way that they can be remodeled to be anything they might like, let alone love. Some homebuyers are moved to tears, as their dream home is revealed. It's so very fun to watch in amazement as these very gifted people envision a dream home from these run-down homes and then make it all happen.

Jenipher, my hairstylist of 32 years, is a very creative person. She can look at any one and style their hair to fit their face. She thinks of each of these hairstyles as art-work. She is really great at color too. She can make you look several years younger. We all know how a great hair-cut and color can make you feel like a million bucks!

When I was young my mom used to crotchet afghans and knit slippers. She used to teach that to my Girl Scout Troop, as she was the leader for a few years. We always enjoyed those, especially in the winter.

My Grandmother and my aunt had a good eye for cloth-ing and putting yourself together. At one time or anoth-er, they both worked at clothing stores and they both really took their time getting the right fit and colors. We all know how a great outfit can also make you look and feel like a million bucks.

Notes:

Creativity Creates Joy

Creativity creates an atmosphere of joy! When we hear a beautiful song, see a beautiful dance, or artwork, it changes our atmosphere to joy. We can also have joy in a newly remodeled home, a great new hairstyle, new clothes, or a great meal; the list goes on.

Psalm 16:11,

"In his presence is fullness of joy!"

Psalm 2:4,

"For he who sits in the heavens laughs!"

Nehemiah 8:10,

"The joy of the Lord is your Strength!"

Proverbs 17:22,

"A merry heart is good like medicine!"

The kingdom of God is about righteousness, peace, and joy! The oil of gladness is joy!

The Fruits of the Spirit are: *love, joy, peace, patience, kindness, goodness, and faithfulness*.

Our Heavenly Father has joy and laughs and we were created in His image; so we are created to laugh and be joyful; to have fun!

You can also have joy in the mists of the storm. One of my sons had to be in the county jail for some minor offenses. The Lord told me in advance this was going to happen. He kept calling me collect and crying. The Lord finally told me that he would be fine and to stop answering the phone. I did what the Lord said, as hard as it was, but in the middle of that storm the joy of the Lord came on me for an afternoon. Although my son was there for another three weeks, I was ok and just like the Lord said, he was fine.

About six years ago, I was diagnosed with In-Situ Breast Cancer. That means the cancer was encapsulated and had not spread. The tumor was so big that they wanted me to have a week of special radiation after surgery, but due to a serious allergy to dye, I was unable to receive that additional week treatment. The doctors wanted me to have the usual 30 day radiation treatments. I did not want to do this but the Lord said He wanted me to. Well-meaning Christians and family wanted me to refuse this treatment, but I knew the Lord's voice so I did what He said. I asked Him why He would want me to do this? He said, "I want you to see the compassion of the radiation therapist." At first, I was getting seriously burned by the radiation. More than the average person, and although the treatment itself didn't hurt, afterwards was terrible. The burns got so bad that they gave me a four day break. The nurses told me they never do that. The Lord said to trust Him and not to worry. He promised me that none of these treatments would have a lasting effect on me. As I began to trust the Lord and notice the compassion of the radiation therapist, a strange, or rather wonderful, thing began to happen. As I would leave the cancer center from these treatments the joy of the Lord would come on me and I would laugh in my car all the way to work. This continued through the last two weeks of my treatments. Eventually the patient who was getting severely burned now didn't even have a scar from radiation treatments. The doctor and the mammogram techs told me that they couldn't believe that I had no scars from radiation. One of the mammogram techs even went so far as to say, "Don't you know that women are deformed from having radiation?" I had no idea. I don't even know if they were Christians, but I hope I can show compassion like that. The joy of the Lord is our weapon. It is our warfare and it is our strength. The joy of the Lord is a good medicine!

Father of Lights

James 1:17

> "Every good and perfect gift is from above, coming down from the Father of lights, who does not change like shifting shadows."

Every good and perfect gift is from above. So if your gifting is creating joy, and that is part of the kingdom of God, it should put a whole new perspective on the importance of doing what you love to do!

I don't know about you, but I love colors and I love flowers. Colors and flowers can have some heavenly meanings. Don't you just love flowers?! Each one has a beauty all its own.

In the Book <u>The Divinity Code; Understanding your Dreams and Visions</u> by Adam F. Thompson and Adrian Beale, they list under the meaning of colors; "The color of clothing and vehicles is a very important indicator of the meanings they carry." Color may communicate: newness, personality and character, splendor, honor, heavenly glory, promise (rainbow), favor, innocence/purity, glory, and may relate to a recent association of someone, something, or someplace using color, and prophetic anointing.

So what if you dressed in colors with purpose or intension? What if you weren't just wearing a blue shirt, but a heavenly blue shirt or prophetic blue shirt? How about a royal purple jacket??

Let me just list a few of my favorites:

Colors:

- White - Holiness and purity

- Yellow - Friendship with God, joy, fun

- Pink - Joy, compassion, sweetness, inner beauty, healing

- Blue - Heavenly, prophetic, revelation

- Green - Life, new life, eternity, abundance, growth, restoration, prosperity

- Purple - Royalty, sonship, inheritance

- Orange - Courage, passion, fire, harvest, strength, boldness, praise

Flowers:

- Daisy - Friendly, happy

- Sunflower - Power

- Tulip - First love

- Lily - Purity, innocence

- Water Lily - Perfect beauty

- Red Rose - Love

- Yellow Rose - Friendship

- Hibiscus - Opportunities

Notes:

The Lord has a Dream

I believe the Lord has a dream for each and every one of us. He is just waiting for us to say yes and come into agreement with His dream. Many of us are pursuing a dream that we have for our lives. God has put a passion in us. That is why we love to sing, dance, play a musical instrument, decorate a home, plant a garden or grow flowers, paint a beautiful painting, or whatever it may be. You may think it is your passion but more than likely, the thing that you love to do, is something that the Lord put in you when He created you! He wants you to do that and have joy in doing it.

A couple of years ago the Lord gave me bits and pieces of little songs. One day, the Holy Spirit told me to put them all together. As I did, I realized this was a whole song and not just several little songs. I love to sing, so here is that song:

Lord, You have a dream

Lord, You have a dream

Lord, You have a dream You want to dream in me

Oh Holy One... Oh worthy One... come and dream Your dream in me

I will seek You, I will praise You with a thankful heart...

Oh Holy One...Oh worthy One

Come and dream Your dream......in ME!

DREAM JESUS' DREAM!

As you sing that song, pretend like you're a princess like Jasmine or Cinderella! And if you're a guy, pretend you're a prince!

Oh, and by the way, the Father loves to hear all of us sing! Our voices are all beautiful to Him. I hear Him say! "Yes!" And I believe He has a giant refrigerator covered with my drawings and paintings, and I bet if you love to draw, yours are on there too!

Notes:

The Beauty of the Lord

The Lord has been speaking to me about His beauty. I have been asking and praying about it. He has put His beauty in each one of us. Each one of us has His glory and His power, which is His beauty, in us. Together each of our pieces creates a beautiful, if you will, mosque painting. A group singing, a group praying, a group serving, and a group dancing - as we individually put our different forms of creativity together, the outcome is beautiful.

Back in Jesus' day, the Pharisees crushed the creativity and beauty in each person. Everyone had to conform to a their way of doing and thinking. They enforced control on those they deemed beneath them. I don't believe that any form of control except for self-control is acceptable. We must never try to control the Holy Spirit in ourselves, nor control others in any way. The root cause of control is fear and a spirit of fear is not from God.

> "God has not given us a spirit of fear but of power, love, and a sound mind."

Today, religious spirits and legalism is what shows up in many churches. Perfection and performance are just two examples of that. That is why we never want to give into perfection and performance.

As I look back on my life, on all the mistakes, all the heartbreaks, all the misunderstandings, all the terrible things others have said and done, and on all the terrible things I've said and done, I see that as I forgave, let go and allowed the Lord to heal me, those all turned into ashes. *The Lord says He will give beauty for ashes.* At one point I had no idea what that meant but now, I think I am finally starting to get a glimpse of what He means. It's okay to want to be excellent for the Lord and do your best for Him, but it's not your job to perfect yourself or anyone else. That is Jesus' job.

Natural Gifts and Spiritual Gifts

There are natural gifts and then there are spiritual gifts. Many people seem to be born gifted with natural gifts such as singing, dancing, art, and so on. Others have a passion in their hearts that have been there since they were very young - they seemed to know they wanted to be a therapist, a doctor, a dentist and so forth, but some just love to cook or host parties. These would be natural, *God-given* gifts.

1 Corinthians 12:4-5,

> "There are different kinds of gifts but the same Spirit. There are different kinds of service but the same Lord."

1 Peter 4:10,

"Each one should use whatever gift he has received to serve others, faithfully administering God's grace in its various forms."

Romans 12:4-7,

"Just as each of us has one body with many members, and these members do not all have the same function, so in Christ we, through many, form one body and each member belongs to all the others."

We have different gifts according to the grace given to each of us. If your gift is prophesying, then prophecy in accordance with your faith, if it is serving, then serve; if it is teaching, then teach.

Romans 12 Gifts Spiritual Gifts

- Exhortation (Encouraging)
- Giving
- Leadership
- Mercy
- Prophecy
- Service
- Teaching

<u>1 Corinthians 12</u>

- Administration
- Apostle
- Discernment
- Faith
- Healing
- Helping
- Knowledge
- Prophecy
- Teaching
- Tongues
- Interpretation of Tongues
- Hospitality
- Wisdom

<u>Ephesians 4</u>

- 5 Fold Ministries
  - *Apostle*
  - *Prophet*
  - *Evangelist*
  - *Pastor*
  - *Teacher*

"Prophetic" means divine heavenly inspiration. You can give a prophetic word in many ways: encouragement, foretelling events, the inspired declaration of divine will and purpose, a prediction of something to come.

If you put the prophetic and a natural gift together you can get prophetic art, prophetic worship, prophetic dance, etc. The ability of the artistic person does not really matter. Although we like to do our best and should, it is not required in order to be used by God. The Lord once told me, "If I tell you to scribble on a piece of paper, it can do whatever I want it to do; it can heal someone!" It can! I have seen it!

Conclusion

Whether we believe in God or not, we are all created in God's image. We all have gifts of creativity inside of us. It just looks different in you than it does in me. Please don't put God in a box and limit what you think creativity is or is not. We are all as individual as a snowflake. God has a dream for each and every one of us. We just need to receive Him as our Lord and Savior, invite Him into our heart, and say **yes to His dream He has for you!** No one else can dream the dream that God wants to dream in **YOU**! You are it....God needs **YOU**!

It doesn't matter how many times you have failed or what your circumstances currently are. Jesus died to take care of ALL of that. You only need to receive what Jesus has done for you! You were born for a time such as this. Our God is the God of the impossible and only He can make a way where there seems to be no way! Trust Jesus! Come and be who you have been created to be!

LET'S PRAY A PRAYER TO RELEASE THE CREATIVITY IN YOU!

Dear Heavenly Father,

We ask for You to release the creativity and the beauty that You have put in me for such a time as this. Holy Spirit, reveal to me each individual area You have gifted me and put a passion in me. I believe I am receiving what I am asking for in Jesus Name! Amen!

Thanks!

It was Kathie Walters who encouraged me to write a book. She felt I was supposed to write a book and helped me do so. It was a similar experience as when the Lord told me to be the artist for The Healing Rooms; I knew that was right even though I didn't understand how it could possibly happen. I know many of you have a book or two in you. I know, because many of you have told me. So don't wait! It's time for you to pick up that pen and write that book, or paint that vision, or whatever it is you feel a passion in your heart to do!

Thank-you Kathie Walters for your encouragement and your nudges along the way to bring out the stories that God has placed in me. It is by the Blood of the Lamb and the word of our testimony!

I would like to thank Patty Foxworth for listening to the Holy Spirit and allowing me to paint in our church's Healing Room, when she had absolutely no other reason to do so.

I would like to thank my husband, Jim Tiefel, for supporting me as I follow the Holy Spirit! Even when I came home with Magenta colored hair, he said, "Wow! Pink! I like it! Just don't do your whole head like that!" Thank-you for encouraging me to be me! You're the best! God knew what He was doing when He put us together.

Most of all, I would like to thank Jesus, my Lord and Savior, my Healer, my Deliverer, my Redeemer; the Lover of my soul. Thank-you for letting me experience You in so many ways! There are no words to express how thankful I am for You and for all that You have done for me!

I would also like to thank Lisa Buck, who did the formatting and cover design for my book. Thank-you for believing in me and going way above and beyond. Without your creativity and vision, my book would still be on my computer.

Cindy Tiefel
Father's Heart Ministry
ctiefel@icloud.com

* 9 7 8 1 8 8 8 0 8 1 2 2 0 *